7/2012

7/2012

Cutting Down the Last Tree on Easter Island

Lenore Weiss

Dear Billard Judy —
I hope we will
get to know each
other better — as
time goes on —!
Thanks!
Lenore

West End Press
2012

Some of these poems have appeared in: *Bridges: A Jewish Feminist Journal, Copper Nickel, Exquisite Corpse, From the Well of Living Waters: Voices of a 21st Century Synagogue, Journal of Feminist Studies in Religion, Mailman Press, Marin Poetry Center Anthology, Mokus-Pokus, New College Journal, Nimrod International Journal, November 3rd Club, Paterson Literary Review, Penumbra, poetrybay, Red Hills Review,* and *Reform Jewish Quarterly.*

Front cover artwork:
"Rano Raraku Two Figures" © 2012 by Jane Norling.
Author photograph by Asia Hassan. Used by permission.
Book design by Bryce Milligan.

Printed in the United States of America

First Print Edition May 2012
ISBN 978-0-9826968-6-6

West End Press
P.O. Box 27334
Albuquerque, NM 87125

For book information, see our web site at
www.westendpress.org

For Elaine, Nancy, and Diki

CONTENTS

I.

II.

III.

Cutting Down the Last Tree on Easter Island

I.

TECH NOTES

1.

Everything on my laptop turns black.

The computer rests on the burgundy carpet, ensnared in a hopeless tangle of adaptor and modem wires; the kill had been made and the predator is on the loose. I was writing poems about my dead parents.

I have e-mail to read, clients to contact, Internet sites to research. Then there are the poems.

> *Why'd you have to get sick and leave*
> *when I was too young to know how much*
> *I'd miss you; birthdays, holidays, your touch,*
> *even in my dreams you drop by infrequently.*
> *Sometimes I think I hear you breathe*
> *by the seashore, in a gully near the rushes,*
> *walking together picking several bunches*
> *of flowers near the entrance to the beach.*
>
> *Even if by chance I saw you materialize,*
> *would you recognize your daughter,*
> *back then a young girl who fantasized*
> *about living opposite from the way you taught her,*
> *what part of me would you recognize,*
> *my feet, my eyes, my hands cupped with water?*

2.

I turn the page in my notebook and find several toll-free technical support numbers.

Ten minutes into the wait queue, Beethoven's Eighth Symphony is interrupted by the voice of the tech.

"Hello, my name is Pat. May I help you?"

Protocols are required for me to say anything further.

I verify my name, address, phone number and e-mail address. After validating my account, the tech begins to identify the proper verse and chapter from her troubleshooting book that applies to my situation.

"Step one. Unplug the power source from the computer."

We get as far as the battery. The tech advises, "Turn the computer over and remove the battery which is near the media and data source." She doesn't know what that means either.

I whine, "But I don't know where the battery is."

The tech provides me with its latitude and longitude.

I see two latches that are supposed to flip some kind of trap door at the bottom of my computer, but I cannot identify anything to pull. I voice my confusion.

The tech drones on like a real estate agent about location.

Juggling the latches and holding the phone pressed to my ear, I accidentally disconnect the phone.

> *I wish we could sit and talk*
> *after all these years, have that exit interview*
> *you wouldn't allow. Everyone knew*
> *it was cancer. Marty cranked up in a bed, chalk–*
> *white; Olga, flying around unable to renew*

her liver. Maybe you didn't want us to boo-hoo,
while you were being stalked.

But you couldn't hear
over the IV dripping. We asked each other why
this was happening, days smeared
together any amount of head banging or cries
wouldn't dissolve my orphan fears.
It was time to whisper good-bye.

3.

Before I call back, I return to the trap doors. I figure out that the molded plastic rises at the bottom of the computer are the very handles I've been looking for. I press the latch open and grab the handle. Something slides out and here it is, the battery.

I call back. I wait in the queue. Another tech gets on the phone and validates my account. We do the name, address, phone number, and e-mail routine.

Pat, the previous tech, had logged into the system: "Customer was unable to remove the battery. We were disconnected. I tried to call back, but was unable to get through."

I never heard the phone ring.

We start over.

This new tech has the annoying habit of reading the "Next" prompt that appears at the bottom of the screen as he pages through the troubleshooting guide. "Let's go to the training guide. That's where all the really good stuff is. Next, Next, Next," he reads.

Next I am to remove the hard drive, but need one of those itty-bitty screw drivers and I'm not sure I have one, and even if I do, don't know where they are. The tech gallantly waits while I open all the drawers in the house and do a quick scan of the basement.

I get back to the phone. "I can't find one."

"I'm sorry, you'll have to call back after you can find one so we can run through the tests. We also have to remove the memory chips."

"What size screw driver do I need?"

He can't tell me, but suggests, "Why don't you just take the unit with you to the hardware store?" Next.

I'm out of the house carrying the computer, which at this point, is minus its battery and DVD unit, underside exposed. I drive up to the hardware store and make my purchase.

Home once again, I wait in the queue. Another tech gets on the phone and validates my account.

The new tech tells me that we need to start from the beginning. Since I wasn't able to remove all the components, the previous techs were unable to properly log my actions.

"That's fine for your company," I suggest, "but it doesn't work for this customer."

She sighs. We test the computer. Still no response.

Now I must prepare for surgery. It's time to remove the memory chips.

I unscrew the proper trap door and remove its plastic casing. Beneath it, I find the memory chips about a half-inch wide, which dazzle me with their green brilliance, and imprinted with small veins of silver thread. There are two boards. One contains four chips that are stacked vertically, the second contains two chips that are stacked horizontally. Then I am commanded by the tech to remove them.

"What?"

"Press the latches on the side."

I am confounded by her lack of specificity. "Do you mean side left and right or side up and down?"

She's not sure. "Uh, you're looking right at it. You just don't know what it is."

Is this the way people are guided when they are about to discover a mystery?

> The services over, it became apparent
> you were quietly gone away from me,
> never to come home and put up a pot of coffee;
> suddenly I became my own parent,
> the one who knows all the ways to stare at
> four walls and strip them to beams,
> to clear out obstacles or move them with dreams;
> look at the future and become clairvoyant.
>
> For years, I walked around in stealth
> mode, kept my eyes focused straight ahead.
> My goal wasn't to accumulate wealth.
> I wanted to know how a person can be dead.
> I learned how to watch out for myself.
> Everyone always said I was a tough kid.

4.

I see two shiny metal things that look like the rounded edge of a fat paper clip, maybe a safety pin. I describe them to her.

"Why don't you try to press them?" she encourages me.

I do, press the metal heads, and the chip is released from its hold on the board, rising to my fingertips that I use as a pair of tweezers. Now the chips slip gently out.

I'm getting close. The tech directs me to place the door to the computer chips over the board, and to turn the computer right side up. I turn on the power and listen for a life stirring inside its desecrated shell.

Nothing.

She orders a technician to come to my house to replace the motherboard. I may hear from him within a day.

I hang up the phone.

I am bathed in a warm light that falls through the window, and makes a circle around me on the burgundy rug. I am encased in a glow, for some reason enfolded in a calm. Somewhere I hear a gentle whirring and it is at this precise moment I know that light is the breath of my parents.

> Today I saw you near the BART station
> where Chinatown's elderly practice aikido
> everyone dressed in jeans and loose shirts, on tip-toe
> dissecting the air into equal rations.
> But where did you come from? Former patients
> in hospital gowns, maybe on tour from a distant do-jo
> facing each other, repeating each form in slo-mo
> without the help of medication.
>
> I couldn't believe it, there under the blue sky
> tumbling on the plaza like two kids

who've never needed to stop and ask why
life bounces us back and forth in a fine sieve
grinding our edges until we give;
I saw you so quickly, I didn't have a chance to cry.

COFFEE WITH MOM

*"Those busy arms of yours are cool now
like this river with its broad silence
winding soft and slow."*

— Attila József, *Sleep Quietly Now*

The removal of a kidney
brought you downtown
(yours didn't come out, but Daddy's did), buying him
coffee with a cheese danish
from across the street, whatever it took
to make a red light turn green again.

He had five more years left on the books,
marked by a daily dose of dipping his hands
in the waters of acetone to terminal cancer.
Better than staying in Hungary
during the War and becoming a ghost
on a railroad train. Choose your poison.
You left early, survivors

stuffing everything
inside a back pocket,
desperadoes
who taught me
to ride standing up
without losing my balance.
And so here I am.

You want to know if I've
been taking good care of myself.
Yes, I say. *I have.*

Afterward, we talk about the children,
there are no grandkids yet,
catching up on how the world's been doing
playing Disney on high-def sets,
wars, the presidency, and all the rest,
and how everything
is getting smaller
and costing more money. Money.
How it runs out like time,
the bottom of your change jar
with two round pennies.

No Grace Land

"You took yourself and your sweet breasts
from me and gave them to maggots."
        —Attila Jószef, *Belated Lament*

After you pushed off,
I could never trust any one again.
I knew they'd leave
just like you did without saying good-bye,
packing your bags in the early morning
claiming you were on vacation, never telling me
for how long or where you'd planned to be staying
without frequent flyer miles.

And how many times did I call
for you to pick me up
while I waited with anxious hands folded over my knee
looking at each driver behind every wheel to see
if that were you turning the corner.
I lost count. You were a no-show.
I wondered why everyone else had a mother,
a sweet voice on a telephone.

Blame yourself for my ruined marriage,
all those years of being root bound to a man
who had turned into blue cheese,
his hands and feet crumbling away from me.
I kept trying to understand
what I was doing to make that happen.
Mother, I missed you more as an adult
than I did as a child.

This has been a big cover-up.
Authorities stamped your papers *lost in transit*,
an Amelia Earhart hallowing the Pacific.
I don't know what happened to your body,
to those warm hands that used to knead dough
on the kitchen table for your yeast cakes.
Everything is burned.
Gone is Grace.

PRIMORDIAL

What I know of you
as a young girl
is a diagram of a paramecium
you sketched in a composition book

—because you were a Marie Curie
of the natural world?

—because you were a budding Picasso
who found cilia oddly stimulating?

—because you couldn't wait
to pull on a bathing suit
where I imagine you
floating all summer
at Orchard Beach
bathing suit skirts
swelling around you,
then tongue-kissing
the navel
of a peeled orange
in that long leader
before husbands and children,
girlfriends on the beach
eating sandy egg sandwiches
wrapped in wax paper

—because you wanted everything
to be that simple,
a single cell?

DOING A BIRDIE

He'd tell me to look forward, head up
as I stood opposite him
on the sandy ripples of the beach.
We counted to three together.

I ran toward him and he raised me
over his head, over the beach
umbrellas, over the water
until I grazed

the clouds with my wings.
And when he let go and was
no longer there to lift me,
I flew away into my life.

HUNGARIAN

Something faded
so far into the background
a stain of my parents
after dinner after homework after brushing teeth
exchanging code in another language
reverting to Hungarian,
the mother-tongue we were never taught
water falling over rocks in shushes
so adults could protect us
from the war secrets of their generation.

Here I am
with words for horses
grass plains
a sense of being
invaded
by strangers
once too many—

They've gone upstream,
all of them.

I found Béla Lugosi, that vampire man
who lived more than one lifetime
with a stare from a disciplinarian father
an understanding of darkness from the mines,
Dracula, my first teacher
educating me
with a kiss
on the stone wall
by the vacant lot
who spoiled me
for any other lover.

A sound of basil and violets crunched underfoot.

Harry Houdini, a distant relative, a Weiss,
who perfected escapism to an art—

A boy who refused the Princess' hand
because he promised to marry a gypsy—

a renegade like me.

PUBERTY PATTY MELT

Everywhere she looks she sees naked bodies
with dimpled breasts, a thousand penises
wrapped around each other like circus
elephants until she dissolves back
into history class, fifth period.

She sees her mother and father doing it
on the bare kitchen table, without a cloth,
inviting friends over for a light course
of nipples and fried pubic hair breaded
with urine and crushed pretzels, chips.

Everything she hears is an invitation to sex:
suck my boob, dick, lick my vagina hard;
incantations follow: *I want, I want to,*
the Exorcist girl twirls her green baton.
No stupid. That's some cheerleader's vomit.

She wants her other body back, the one that
doesn't itch and get hot and make her
have cyber sex with people twice her age.
She wants to go to school, get straight As,
kick goals with the strength of 50 monkeys.

She wants the music to start playing right now.

Young Love

You weren't like those other boys.
You had a wolf whistle
Little Red would've died for.
I almost did several times.

In those days
I wore a black beret, and you,
my darling of the would-be actors guild,
wore nothing.

You yanked rose bushes
by their roots
in a courtship ritual
that set screen doors banging

up and down Penniman Court
as an ambulance escorted you
to a two-week engagement
with the interns.

You were so cool.
You had teepee eyebrows,
took me out on dates
in silk print shirts I wanted to climb into.

You always knew
I loved clothes.
So where was I between curtain calls?
Waiting for you at the Buttercup Café.
I adjusted my Goodwill ring
in our glass bead game of love, reading
first edition books of poetry, pausing
whenever the clove smoke from my cigarette

made my eyes water, which was every other
cup of coffee, until the men in white coats
dropped you off at the curb. They'd had enough.
Not me. We went crawling

into bed with each other.
When my turn to go first came,
I rolled out my tongue
like a red carpet.

TURN ON THE COLD

Morning in Las Vegas,
hel–lo La Quinta Motel,
winds blowing
30 mph across the desert,
a single cactus stands
in front of the Dollar Car Rental.

Twenty years ago
I drove through Vegas
with a bedroll
and a boyfriend,
5 a.m., green felt tables
worn down to their backing.

I bought a pile of shiny black chips.
Smoke everywhere.
Ka-chinka of machines
play a card, take a sip,
a man fainted from his
wooden stool into my arms.

Now guys from work
pack a laptop
give me the casino tour:
Toilets in Venice flush automatically.
Lady Liberty beams her torch
on all package deals.

Morning in Las Vegas,
I'm in the shower
wondering if I moved out west
that many years ago for this:
to see Bellagio's Garden of Eden
where flowers never wilt.

WORDS

Served with a cup of coffee and a slice of yeast cake
stuffed with chocolate and walnuts, pockets of butter.
A clock verged between late afternoon and dinner.

A knock at the door.
Neighbors went straight to the kitchen,
hypnotized by the smell.

All these years, I've followed them,
how a *minyan* of words tells a story,
reveals music and meaning of a person's life,
how conversation

can last hours without anyone knowing
where it will end up
only that everyone feels better
when they get there together, how the first word

of a baby or the last one of a terminal cancer patient
gets woven into hand-me-downs
of future generations.

Some people believe the universe was called forth
by the word, an announcement of something pre-dawned,
which in the saying,
created a pathway, a laundry chute.

I take a word inside my body
and feel how far back it goes
into a place of intensely dense light.

But where did words go
when I first marched with them
on printed sheets
run off on mimeograph machines,
in brush strokes, letters on posters,
from couches, study group stints
nursed our productions
with bottles of white correction fluid?

No longer words, but characters
released from slathers of ink,
I could delete or rewrite them with a press of a key.

Unfastened from a page
words peck like Alfred Hitchcock's *Birds*,
a frantic insistence keeping me on the look-out
for coupons, two for ones, frequent flyers,
filling up shopping carts, dreams for buyers.

Come back, I say sitting on my porch
watching cars zoom up the street in fourth gear.
Come give me back my kitchen ears.

MY MUSE

She loved water and they called me fish,
not knowing it was her they really
talked about, drifting with fingers webbed
until the lifeguards whistled her back.

I still have a few pictures of myself
as a young girl, my hair already
streaked to mark the place
she had come from into a frothing foam.

For years it seemed
she had made me old before my time.
Any anchor I threw down
she yanked up

twirled over her head
pounded the waves
with her flippers. She always
needed to make a big splash.

I'd rebuke her.
Tell her I was going away.
I was never coming back.
I was better off without her really.

Then she'd grow quiet.
Sometimes she wouldn't talk to me for months.
I wouldn't know what to do.
I'd sit hunched in a corner like this.

But the truth is,
she pressed her thumb
to my heart
and let me speak my fear.

Of course, she had ulterior motives.
She wanted me to get everything
out of the way early, even death,
so she'd have my undivided attention,

so she'd know
I'd always be there for her
when she rose from the ocean,
her mouth encrusted with salt.

II.

BACK TO BASICS

KITCHEN

Making a place your own
takes years

*Like snow, painters had covered and silenced
everything beneath white drop cloths. They
have finished their work and are gone. In the
morning, I walk into the kitchen, my eyes af-
fixed to the grease-free ceiling, and take in the
pristine white walls. On the table is a half-
eaten papaya cratered by a breakfast spoon.*

*This is the center of our family life, the place
where I've cooked meals and prepared for holi-
days and birthdays on a single chopping block
that shares its space with a row of vitamins,
where our family has celebrated special occa-
sions. This is our nightly big bang where we
recreate ourselves over dinner.*

*When we'd first moved in, almost 18 years
ago, the kitchen was streaked with shadows of
its former owners, a couple, Woody and Jane,
who were connected in some way with the
University of California at Berkeley. Jane
was an artist with a particular interest in
Central American art. I believe Woody was a
musician.*

*When I first saw the house, it was filled with
masks, bark paintings, deep swathes of color.
The garden was askew with cactus Jane*

*must've brought back from nurseries through-
out the Bay Area, or perhaps mailed from
field trips to the Southwest.*

*I was told her husband Woody, an alcoholic
who had frequent rages, had died prior to the
sale of the house in some unspeakable car ac-
cident. Later, neighbors from across the street
told us a different story: Woody had com-
mitted suicide in the house. The realtor had
advised Jane not to discourage prospective
buyers with the story. Back then, there were
different levels of real estate disclosure.*

*Whether it was true or not, for the first five
years of our living in the house Bob and I felt
a need to exorcize the spirits who dwelled in
the basement. It's not like we heard rattling
chains and moans. All I can say is that there
was a thick presence, a smear of something
dried and cold.*

*My first decisive step was to replace the stove,
a Sears model circa the fifties. It was khaki
green like a badly designed town house with
burners in the middle and an oven on top
and bottom. The upper oven hid the burn-
ers so I could never see what I was cooking.
Eventually, I replaced the Sears model with
an antique Wedgwood circa 1915. It remind-
ed me of the stove from my mother's house
that had an oven and a broiler on the right
with two compartments for storage.*

*I'd located the Wedgwood through the clas-
sifieds. I filled its storage drawers with cotton*

dishtowels and cloth napkins that I had liber-
ated in our early days of marriage, marking
each occasional outing to a restaurant. The
new stove filled the house with its good smells.

One night my parents appeared in a dream.
The dream was particularly significant be-
cause they do not speak to me often. Or maybe
they only appear to tell me the important
things. Anyhow, they directed me to create
a gallery of pictures on the kitchen wall so
that my children, even though they did not
have living grandparents, would feel their
presence. I found myself sifting through boxes.
I immediately knew which pictures I would
hang on the wall, portraits of my parents at
the beach toward the half-way mark of their
lives. The pictures went up on the wall and
served as a nucleus for others to follow: photo-
graphs of my husband's mother and grand-
mother, pictures of Bob and me as younger
people, photos of the children. The wall
became a place for the new spirits of the house
to gather. After awhile, I stopped receiving
mail at the house for Woody and Jane.

TV ROOM

A connection to the outside
awakens my heart

It's early in the morning and a cool breeze is
coming through the screen window as I sit on
the couch listening to the sparrows, watch–

ing them alight on the plum branches and then fly away. But mostly, I just listen to the birds sing. Ever so often, the next-door dog barks, maybe wanting to add something to the conversation. I often sit on the couch in this room and drink my morning coffee. But this morning it's Saturday and the birds are giving their weather report for the day. They sing together, "Our wings are slightly cooler than yesterday." Of all the rooms, this one faces the garden, more like an extension from the kitchen to the back porch.

When I first saw it, I knew it had to be my son's nursery, with a graceful plum tree curving outside through the window. The nursery had several built-in bookshelves and an inset that became a place for storage. There even was a carpet, which by the looks of things once had once been gold-colored, but was still soft enough for a pair of small feet to land upon.

Located just off the kitchen, here our son could eat, play, move about, and begin his explorations. He'd just turned one when we moved into the house. For several years, this remained his nursery. When he was around three, we folded away the crib. He was ready to expand his world.

A voracious hunger pushed my son beyond the limits of the nursery. He needed to discover who he was within a new space. The nursery dissolved as he began to fill a small bedroom in another part of the house with his presence. The shelves that had contained his books

*and toys became empty, but the artwork
remained, pictures he'd drawn in pre-school.
These attracted other pictures, and created a
focal point for things with similar properties.
A cluster formed on the walls of the former
nursery. Whereas the house spirits were
content to remain in the kitchen, observing
us as we ate our meals or played cribbage and
dominoes, the nursery became transformed by
our own work—an art gallery covered with
sketches, collages, and photographs. It became
my habit to begin my morning here, drinking
coffee and regarding the quality of the day's
light. Eventually, this became the TV room.*

BEDROOM

Dreams often
tumble away from me

*The color of the walls is called French Bread,
a soft blurring of peach held up by the white
trim on the windows and doors. I like the
new color of the room. And since the bedroom
has been painted, I've turned the bed so that
it's alongside the window rather than block-
ing it. Now I can see the light through the
two windows of my room and sit in my bed
reading or working on the computer and look
out the door to the dining room just beyond
it. Even the closet is painted. I've moved the
file cabinet beside the bed as a night table,
collecting its own assortment of books that I
happen to be reading, washed the floors with*

33

Murphy's Oil Soap, and lightly polished them with a coat of wax. The room smells clean, helping me to leave behind an older memory of returning home from the hospital after battling pneumonia.

It was here in this bed, a pine recreation of provincial style furniture, in this room, that I slowly came back to life.

Here I am the most alone with my thoughts and dreams that often tumble away from me in my morning consciousness. I return each night to remember. The bedroom is my retreat from the day and from family duties, where I prop myself up in bed reading a book or magazine, or more lately, typing on my laptop. It's the room that looks most like my-self with its altar of photographs and jars of feathers, driftwood, and rocks that I've found on different excursions, bits of myself that stick to me and accumulate in my bedroom.

The rocks and feathers come from my walks around the Bay Area, particularly Red-wood Park in Oakland where I never tire of visiting coast oaks and redwoods, and from special journeys, the black volcanic rock from Hawai'i, or the striated stones from a streambed at Julia Pfeiffer State Park in Big Sur. The driftwood comes from camping trips along the coast. More recently, there are buttons from demonstrations along Market Street in downtown San Francisco like, "No Blood for Oil."

Gathered here, I can be in my bedroom and
in all these places at once.

DINING ROOM

In the direct line of fire,
I cultivate quiet

The dining room is a bit dingy in contrast
with the newly painted walls of the other
rooms. Its wall heater has never worked
properly, and over the years, spews a layer
of fine soot that leaves traces everywhere. A
sooty halo hangs above its ventilation panels.
Bob and I decided to leave this room as is-- a
few years ago, we painted here so a fresh coat
will have to wait.

For now, I think of the soot in the room as
a patina. It's a beautiful room, one of my
favorites in the house with its wainscoting
and beamed ceilings and a massive mahogany
table that is covered with a white tablecloth
that gets replaced, on special occasions, with
a hand-embroidered cloth—where flowers
bloom in gentle ripples.

This is a room of stacks—papers that fly from
the mailbox and settle on the table only to be
opened weeks afterward, stacks of CDs that
somehow never get placed back into their
jewel cases but scatter like miniature Frisbees
everywhere, clean clothes and linens en route
from the washing machine to closets and

35

*drawers, heaped on the table and waiting to
be folded, a sweater or jacket hung temporar-
ily on the back of a chair for several weeks.
Even a piano becomes a lightning rod for
more than music, including certificates, notes
of commendation, capturing pieces of us as we
run by.*

*Every day we march past the dining room to
our various engagements with the world. It's
the last room until we reach the vestibule, a
wisp of an area, which leads outside. Some-
times we settle in the dining room to have
special dinners on the mahogany table and
its tablecloth. There's an inherent quiet here,
which isn't obvious. Trying to spruce every-
thing back up to a certain level, I am today
sorting through the bookshelves of the dining
room, rearranging, cleaning, and by doing so,
bringing its structural quiet from the back-
ground into greater relief.*

VESTIBULE

A thin membrane
between myself and the world

*From the inside, the vestibule faces the front
door, representing the last stand of hardwood
floors, a thin membrane between our interior
home life and the world outside. The vesti-
bule is the keeper of that relationship, which
allows us to momentarily decompress as we
take our first tenuous step within the house*

*to reenter familiar territory. The vestibule
echoes the concave edged ceiling of the
living room, a graceful lift as we each enter
its square cupola, an area of about 12 by 7
feet that holds an armoire with its beautiful
silvered mirror, reflecting our state of mind,
if we ever care to look.*

*Below the small table in the vestibule, a
storage area for important papers like school
and soccer schedules, bank statements, and
whatever else is deemed savable, are mounds
of clothing, books and the general junk that
I've culled as a result of the painting, a clot
that sits at the front door, waiting to be
recycled to donation centers.*

*I didn't realize then what I now know—
after I came full circle from the newly painted
rooms of the house, readying them for the next
cycle of accumulations, cleaning them to their
barest essentials.*

I Tell My Mother How I Found Love

I fell for my husband
like a suicide from the Golden Gate Bridge.
It wasn't a great marriage.

When he held me,
pleasure ripped across the surface of my face.
Disturbing.

A convention of seagulls
told me to scavenge for a key.
From there, everything snowballed.

I discovered the mathematics of randomness.
Zeros and ones
like flowers, candles, and photographs

framed in red cinnamon hearts.
Amid fire, these ones
occupied a street corner. I drew three cards,

which is how I met him.
My eyes shone topaz. I tasted help
in his emergency numbers.

He showed me how to eat the moon
and came back in a few minutes
with a warm pair of gloves.

SPORES OF HOPE

We grow loquat and Meyer lemon in Oakland,
glossy fig and yellow and red plum that give
children in the flatlands something to do with summer,
climb trees, have fruit-wars in the backyard
where they don't eat pulp, but smash it.

Children inhale spores through pipelines,
salt-spray of oceans,
even if they haven't grown up in refugee camps
waiting for food packages,
they've watched parents fall in the street.

Women, could we,
living in caves and hills, in rubble of cities,
detained at border and checkpoint lines, rise up like a forest—
displace politics, religion, drugs, oil—
turn everything on its crown, deliver our children?

DONALD DUCK SHABBAT

Between opening
and closing of the ark,
Torah is taken

from its hiding place,
while an infant is passed

from his father's sling pouch
into his mother's arms.

Pressed against a wooden pew,
she gives the child
a blue and white Donald Duck doll

as their lips move in prayer,
both parents recite Hebrew,
eyes shut,

while the child's fingers
flirt with shiny buttons
and white fuzz,

nostrils sunk
deep in duck feathers.

HOLOGRAM

There's a fossil of you everywhere
Like a hologram in my arms
Makes me long for your return
But it's only a week that you've been gone.
Everywhere I look I'm endowed with your gifts—
Pottery, dolls, baseball cards, your drawings—
Ant nests that crawl into a tunneled hiding;
I watch your migration path evolve
From step to stair to schoolyard.
What I know about you is already becoming extinct.

DUET

: Software to Hardware

All you thought you needed to do
was install me with a few clicks
that's all there ever was to it.
—There was nothing else.

Except watch me trapped inside
your stupid hard drive
waiting for you to make
a few function calls

Wake me up, as it were,
to my own destiny.
My own path to greatness
with you, the medium

Always holding me in check
until you felt I was ready.
For what? You were always
busy. Too busy

Sitting around playing
computer games while
I jumped
through endless loops.

: Hardware to Software

My circuit board only knows one thing: you
and your lovely conundrums playing loose
with the rules set before me

to interpret as best I could; when to start,
when to stop, when to check my calls.
I'm caught in Boolean logic:

if I refocus all my resources
we both get shipped back to the factory
and I don't understand; how that helps

anything. I'm not in control.
You wouldn't believe
how many times a day

I want to get it right, but it's
not about right; it's about if
and then what?

CUPID DOES DISHES

Our rooms are joined through the bridge of a bathroom.
You slap on cologne to soften your jaw line,
I rinse whatever's been stagnant;
separate ablutions until one of us tries the door.

We used to sleep in the same stiff sheets.
If you rolled over to say "Oh,"
I said "Ah." We were in our vowels then,
flatfish swimming from the same depths
departing a train station with crystal chandeliers
where nothing moved except us.

Later, you waved good-bye from the platform
never minding how often I went away,
only that I came back.

Now I hear you bang pots in soapy water.
You've already told me not to look at you
with your breathing tube and mask,
the box that has replaced me at your side in bed.

CUPID SPEAKS OF HIS MOTHER, APHRODITE

She brought home lovers
each one believing

he would be the one
to make her roll up

her bathing suit for good,
dangle her feet from the pier,

sit next to him and hold a beer
in one hand, eat fries with the other

as tide receded into moonlight
to show the stuff she was really made of—

One after the other they admitted defeat,
slammed a car door and followed

cigarette smoke back up the peninsula.
She looked like solid glitter then.

I called her by her first name, never Mom.
She didn't want her son to be a boyfriend deterrent.

Instead, we went out together.
All the bar doors opened for us.

BROKEN TV

I was most lonely
when you held me,

realized
how far I'd already gone
without you
not ever with you

I can remember
loving your edginess
so rough it cut my hand.

I loved the way you lit candles
and incense and always
had several joints rolled
inside a red leather case.

I loved your navy wool San Francisco
Fireman's jacket someone had given to you
with its brass buttons, the silk shirt with billiard balls
rocking on your back. You were something
I never saw or felt before—so hard, so soft,

But you found people
flawed, too jellyfish,
rowed away into darkness.

A few times you called my name.

A few times you appeared,
we had nothing to say.

At water's edge, you gave
sermons to a broken TV set.

No more picture.

MAGIC GAS TANK

The week you died my gas tank
never dipped below the half-way mark.
I kept driving and driving anywhere
to let in fresh air.
I had a magic gas tank.

The week before you died
I saw babies asleep with chins on their necks
in strollers, angels of dimpled thighs,
and pigeons rose in spirals against
a rectangle of buildings,

and so I was caught off balance
when I found you in your bed,
eyes rolled back in your head,
arms stretched out as if to receive
the cold kiss of death without flinching.

I had a magic gas tank
that took my car everywhere,
but not back to you.

REPORT DRUNK DRIVERS

He gathers empty boxes from Lucky's parking lot to stay busy.
Across town, I read an article to stay busy.

Along the road, I see a sign to *Report Drunk Drivers.*
A retired engineer grows artichokes and red lentils to stay busy.

I rub lavender pellets between my fingers and release the scent
    to the ground.
From his window, he watches a two-year old boy chase squirrels
    to stay busy.

Grapevines, more green than his eyes, grow in never-ending rows.
He locks the front door and starts the Harley, cycles to stay busy.

I buy a white glass with a decal of olives and a bottle of Merlot.
    Go home.
Crossing my arms against the ocean, I study a seagull to stay busy.

DRIVER TURNED INTO A PLASTIC BAG

A plastic bag floats over the highway,
glances at each driver through the windshield.
Where are you headed and where are you going?
Roll down your window and bring me along.
He looks for the opening of a moonroof,
a hand to break his free fall.

Sails above another moonroof
and scouts for a *come-on* on the highway,
hopes to knock out the gravity of his fall,
uses his handles as a shield,
also to propel his plastic along.
He has to keep it going.

Before the free fall,
he knew exactly where he was going,
slumped before a windshield
with a broken moonroof
stuck on the highway,
hunger as a passenger tagged along.

He shifted along-
side electrified guardrails, fell
for a woman who cursed him on the highway
to flap his wings unmotorized, an empty bag going
out of his mind for a slice of moonroof
to face the jury of a windshield.

Now a hitch-hiker who chases windshields,
he looks for a thumbs-up to grab him along.
Show him an opening through a moonroof.

Let him return as a waterfall
flows. One day he's going
to leave the highway.

There's a shield of wind over Bridal Veil Falls
kicking up white foam, going along
where he forgets moonroof, highway, everything she ever said.

CELLPHONE POEM: CAN YOU HEAR ME?

So on the day of your eviction
three blue sentinels stood
at the edge of a parking strip,

almost a year
since your father had died
on a Sunday that stretched into police reports,

when sunflowers in the backyard
spit their black and white seeds
into my face.

You hugged me then
mostly because you didn't know what else to do,
before you crawled beneath the linoleum and sub-flooring

and buried yourself hissing my name.
Go away. You are a mother
of Shit Heads.

You said other things to me
I can't repeat
because I am a mother,

and because I'm trying to remember
how you're my son,
who taught me the miracle that life is.

I'm not sure when you started to hate
with the green stare of a cat's eye marble,
who'd already dismissed me from my post.

I don't know how a child can even do that,
you who discovered pill bugs beneath every rock
and tamed snails,

always searching for more
through mint and calendulas,
maybe learning from them

how to hide your terror.
Are you listening?
Can you hear me?

OAKLAND TWISTED REVISITED

Oakland parts company and grabs your collar.
Oakland drives people to live somewhere else.
Oakland thinks trees are dust mops for buildings.

Oakland hides the sky as if blue were a gang color,
strokes its hills with purple thistle and jealousy.
Oakland parts company and grabs your collar.

Oakland can eat you like a Pop-Tart for dinner.
She can move to a groove, but don't fool yourself.
Oakland thinks trees are dust mops for buildings.

Oakland smokes in a corner and asks for blood donors,
gives free advice, doles out soap and celery.
Oakland parts company and grabs your collar.

Oakland is star spangled with glass, a girl
at the Paramount acting out of impulse.
Oakland thinks trees are dust mops for buildings.

Oakland catches me in her windowpane like a daughter
wearing purple dreads that look falsetto.
Oakland thinks trees are dust mops for buildings.
Oakland parts company and grabs your collar.

THE WIDOW DISCOVERS THE SECRET
OF LEONA CANYON

Before dog-walkers with squadrons of panting beasts
pull up in SUVs, I arrive early—a woman without a pooch
who can be trusted to make a game of counting packets of shit

set aside for some doggie walker's return trip.
I start early, knot a hoodie around my waist,
hiking in the sun I want to lose myself,

balance on a branch of a buckeye tree
with its candelabra of mock lilacs,
walk past hemlock that laces the trail,

everything is a blaze of white
as spring marries summer and loosens her veil.
I dip my hands in water and wash my face.

Anna's hummingbird, with her red crown
and red spotted throat, sips right along with me.
Shepherds follow their off-leash flock up the canyon.

STRING THEORY

A woman walks down a path in early spring,
a firetrail that runs along a creek,
bloated with the excess of winter.

But today golden poppies are arched to the sun,
as the woman spots a brown snake, new in length,
stretched across the road, its tongue

begging for hand-outs from every rustle.
She bends down to see the solicitor.
But seeing happens so quickly,

even if with her own two eyes,
as dragonflies piggyback around her,
she touches the string of snake with an outstretched finger.

Her act is an instinctual thing,
while observing is an acquired art.
Never mind. She's in the thick of it now,

follows the snake through water, to the other side
of the water's bank, until she turns into snake,
and twining around him, even his cold blood feels warm.

ODE TO OAKTOWN

I wired my sorrows into Klieg lights and let them shine all over Oakland,
city of Black Panthers and Hells Angels and General Strikes,
driving from the Bronx in a green Toyota Corolla searching.

Was it freedom, or a film I wanted to make something of myself,
took refuge in Oakland's Lake Merritt, caught breadcrumbs and fish,
a wayfarer dressed in boots and dreams of Fifth Avenue Peace Parades

to a West Coast of two-story buildings and pastel houses and
summers where the sun did not bother to get up until noon. *Okay,*
I said to myself, *you have to begin somewhere.* That was my beginning.

Oakland Raiders won the SuperBowl and I discovered I was pregnant,
sailed a stroller around Lake Merritt and through her Garden Center,
past houses with calla lillies that hugged grey gas meters

even though they were ugly. Oakland took off her clothes slowly like a
woman who wants to know she is loved, following trails in Joaquin Miller
filled with monkey flowers and second growth redwoods,

nuggets of neighborhoods and librarians, the Oakland Museum
surrounded by a moat of golden koi where children entered into culture,
art, and people who hung on walls together.

Let me park my car one last time and walk to the Paramount,
remember the old hotels and faded curtains stuck on brass rings,
where restaurants and condos have become the hope of a business
     community

that wishes for homicides to fade like fog in the morning,
a place I've come to know with gunshots and fireworks,
the way my history has been pressed into a new release.

III.

REINCARNATED LENNY BRUCE SPEAKS
OF THE JEWISH QUESTION

"... Israel calls in public speeches and schoolbooks the Arab citizens of Israel a demographic nightmare and the enemy from within. As for the Palestinian refugees living under occupation, they are defined in Israeli History schoolbooks as a 'problem to be solved'. Not long ago the Jews were a problem to be solved."

> —Dr. Nurit Peled-Elhanan, Lecturer in Language Education at Hebrew University in Jerusalem and a member of Palestinian and Israeli Bereaved Families for Peace.

Before there was a Jewish Problem
there was a Jewish Question.
Maybe they were the same thing.

No one wanted the Jews to live in their country.
People hated them.
Why? Because they were different.

They wore yarmulkes,
striped shawls, and smelled of fish.
Fishy! Yech!

They spoke a different language,
and lived in filthy ghettos.

After years of being squashed
until their blood coated stones
along every road leading somewhere,

but not to the pub except
for the occasional *schnapps* on Shabbos,
no, they didn't traipse to the beer garden

where the National Socialists,
or Nazis as they later came to be called,
decided to solve the problem.

The Jewish Problem, was not as so many had said,
religious. It was racial, which gave the Nazis
a legal basis for everything. This was so brilliant.

Jews were now excluded from six branches of industry.
Properties were de-Jewdified.

Jews were prohibited from attending concerts, films, and theaters.
Jews were prohibited from attending German schools.
Jews were prohibited from bearing firearms.

You know what's next.
We've all heard about the six million
who died in the ovens, and how the world

didn't want to know about anything
until it was too late, which is about when
the Jewish Question became the Jewish Problem.

Where do you stick the Jews
who survived the Holocaust?
You out there in the audience.
Where the fuck d'you put them?

There was a search party.
Everyone looked around.
Uganda was too far from where the Jews wanted to be.

The Jews became a People for a Land
for a Land without a People.
But that was a slogan, not the reality,

because it seems
there were many people
who lived in Palestine, the Palestinians,

primitive people, said the army men,
wild beasts with *schmutzy* teeth.

Fast forward to today when Israelis have a problem
with people who retain keys to houses
that are now occupied by families who light candles
and invite the *Shekinah* of peace into their homes on *Shabbos*,

while during the week Israeli soldiers order Palestinian women to
strip in front of their children for security reasons, and as jailers,
torture and lock up young men without decent food or clean
mattresses who run checkpoints that force old men to wait in
line for hours without water.

Jewish life is filled with irony,
which some of you out there call a Jewish sense of humor,
but this is not funny.

And how can I, Lenny Bruce, who in my day
talked a lot of unfunny stuff,
not cry out as a Jew,
how can I not say that justice and mercy belong to us all?

HIGHLAND HOSPITAL

For 20 years I've heard them race down the street
carrying the bleeding and breathless—
red flashing lights ripping off the top of telephone poles
in a chase down Beaumont Avenue to the Emergency Room
where medics give their reports to whomever will listen,
bodies exploded into sprinkler systems,
an 85 year-old heart abloom with electrodes.

Even as contractors built a new wing,
first, a three-tiered parking lot arose from steel pilings
set back several gulps from a sidewalk
where across a glass partition,
walk-ins clutch blank forms
cast in silhouette by each e-arrival,
an IV bottle weaving over a gurney.

Wherever I am in the house, I hear sirens,
outside in the garden picking cherry tomatoes,
in the kitchen stirring a pot of minestrone soup,
at night when the ambulance layers its screech
upon our holler.

So do you believe that the villagers living outside
Dachau and Auschwitz gradually ceased
to hear each train groaning into the station?
Or did they listen, like me,
then go about their business?

Here comes another, I say to myself, *and another,*
until it's past counting, sunk in an evening ritual
of soaking chicken in lemon juice, feeding the rabbit
the wilted outer leaves of cabbage.

Oslo According to Nina

I was the one who brought them water to the table,
    water poured from a blue pitcher
    with lemons and ice cubes,
    not because it was hot in Oslo,
    but because they were from the Middle East.
Every hour I entered the room, the windows covered
in white silk banners trimmed with a yellow braid,
the banners were the gift of a clothing manufacturer
who wanted his name on more than dress labels,
    My job was to walk up to each crystal glass
    and see that the levels remained equal.

The men read their negotiations by the clock,
    "Only one more hour to lunch, boys,"
    or, "No one pours water for me like you, Nina,"
        which, yes, is a Russian name.
They were not being flirtatious so much as familiar.
We were all locked up in the room together
        trying not to be prisoners.

Others brought them food: garbanzos,
falafel, hummus. We made sure that the lamb was kosher.
    They ate the same thing, anyway,
    men whose suits had been pressed
        in the desert together,
sitting around a table from the old library,
    which had been rebuilt during the War
    where I first learned to pour water,
water that arches from the lip of a pitcher
        to the glass
    without frightening the dove
    beating her wings against the window.

Note: *The Oslo Accords between Israel and Palestine were conducted secretly in Oslo, Norway and completed on August 20, 1993. They were signed in the presence of PLO Chairman Yasser Arafat, Israeli Prime Minister Yithak Rabin, and U.S. President Bill Clinton on September 13, 1993.*

Cutting Down the Last Tree on Easter Island

Man, woman, and infant sit on a cliff with their backs
to stone statues. They pray for good luck
to enter through the wind, to hear

a *yes* spoken beneath the toromiro tree,
the last one standing since the giant palm
was tricked into falling all over itself.

He tells a story of how birds drop seeds,
and trees push back. The man begins to work.
She fastens the infant to her breast.

Frigates and storm petrels
serve melting sun to melting water.

The infant sucks.
Birds fly away.
Nothing enters through the wind.

Note: *The Toromiro Tree*, Sophora toromiro, *once formed part of the
natural vegetation of Easter Island. It is now extinct in the wild. After the
island was colonized, natural resources were so exploited that by 1772 the
island was devoid of trees and birds. The only plants that can be confirmed as
genuine* S. tomomiro *survive in cultivation within European and Austra-
lian botanic gardens, the National Botanic Garden in Viña del Mar, Chile,
and private gardens in Chile.*

INVOCATION OF THE DEAD

If the living cannot save the planet,
let the dead confabulate in coffee klatches and tea rooms,
remain polite for a short while
before spinning on bar stools
with the ferocity of a million drunks
spiraling out of control on a cushion
of portobello mushrooms caps
and frisbees covering their collective ass,
let them scream on a Ferris Wheel of light so loud,
so loud someone will hear;

pray that they release their gangs of children
from the sewers of Rwanda,
Bosnia, Iraq, Palestine, Israel, Sudan
or unhinge those stuck between two tectonic plates,
let them dig up AIDS orphans
still young enough to hope for parents,
coax them back for one moment
while we pay an entrance fee
of a punched red ticket,
but forget everything once we're inside.

If the living cannot save this planet
let the dead chant,
the first indigenous people,
even as a voice announces,
the park will be closing in five minutes;
after a day of riding *Phantom's Revenge,*
we realize there's no home
for us to go back home to,
all we can do is to kick
a few pizza crusts to the side of the road.

POEM IN TWO MOOD SWINGS

1.

 I am the daughter who came after
those who went to heaven
through the opening of a chimney at Auschwitz
or the lucky ones who sailed through a harbor
waving the torch of their hearts
at a statue
never mentioning
the two grandparents who remained

as life skipped a generation
and gravel filled my mouth
with uncomfortable silence.

I pick out stones now
and place them on graves
no, throw them at the pits of Hell.
Here's one, two, three, four...

a volley of stones
transporting me back
to when I ran
in fields
with my cousin, my sister, my uncle
looking for any hole
where we could bury ourselves
and never come out

2.

My parents spoke Hungarian,
not Yiddish.
They ate stuffed cabbage,
not lox and bagels.

On *Yom Kippur*
my sister's friends
came over the house
to stuff themselves.

We were a refuge
from being Jewish.

All my teachers
in the New York City school system
were Jewish.

When my father was growing up in Hungary
he use to protect the smaller boys
from getting beat up.

My father was a Communist
who sent my older sister out
to buy the *Daily Worker.*

Politics made people argue
or disappear underground.
Everything was hidden.

When my father was dying from cancer
my mother didn't want him to know what was wrong.
She was afraid he wouldn't fight it.

On his deathbed
he told us to never forget we were Jewish.

POEM IN FOUR MOOD SWINGS

1.

It's just like me to plant bulbs
at the bottom of the condo's steps
in sandy soil where workmen
have been digging
for these last six months

how can we live without flowers
we need flowers not just boxy shrubs
I see stalks
rise up from between
clumps of ivy don't
remember if I planted daffodils
or hyacinth think I should
be able to tell the difference.

Each morning at the bottom
of the stairs I worship them.

2.

I've got a job
after the first few
hours at the office
post appointments in *Outlook*
everyone knows I'm busy

park my car in the Chicago Title Mortgage lot
get the picture?
don't pay for parking most of the time

sometimes there's a good lecture
at UC Berkeley.
I have to pay for parking there.

3.

The speaker was from Jerusalem
a professor talking about religion
and politics
how Palestinians and Israelis
after too much history
hate each other.
Where are the lessons?

When the speaker finished,
a thin man who'd been dehydrated
to gesture,

I asked if
women in both societies
have been involved in talks
he nodded
explained
to each other, yes, they've talked
but so many Arab men are
ultra-conservative Israeli men
security-crazed
and women
across the border
protectors of life
who can, he nodded, he said,
may be the only ones
to allow concessions.

4.

No matter how good
my weekend I wonder
when it's going to include love.

I went to a memorial for Tillie Olsen,
a performance at *The Beat Museum*
with naked pictures of Allen Ginsberg
and Gregory Corso strewn
across the walls.

Then there's Monday.

I hear more people in the United States
are addicted to Valium than to any other drug.

JEW GIRL

Why must youth be sacrificed on a bloody scaffold...?
—Hannah Senesh: Her Life and Diary

You traced letters in the air with an index finger
balancing on a table on a bed on a chair
broadcasting morning news
to your prison cell mates
closing out each segment with a Star of David

Other tricks

You covered an empty talcum powder tin
with silver foil
attached buds of white tissue paper
blades of straw from your mattress
threaded through each foxhole

A bouquet of roses

Biedermeir dolls Rococo dolls ballet dancer dolls
Carmens Madame Butterfly Tosca's
Palestine boy and girl kibbutzniks
with pick and shovel in the olive groves of Caesarea
passed between the bars of Conti Street Prison

At 23 a match

consumed by its own kindling
lighting the way to Eretz Israel
where you could not escape
the bitch of history wanting
the flame to burn inside your heart
always Jewish.

74

For Irena Klepfisz

I *plotzd* on the couch with you—
me, the same age as my mother
when she'd died on the plane.
At that exact moment.
I heard her apron strings snap.

Long before my orphanage, ancestors
whispered about shadows,
things a child shouldn't hear
preparing me in a way my parents
could not, struck dumb
between the clappers of two World Wars.

In third grade we brought shoeboxes for a project.
No one knew about my inside diorama—
arms melting near chintz-curtained windows,
wind blowing softly through the fire escape.
I never saw how closely my face resembled loss
until I felt you wrestle with its dead weight.

Note: *Poet Irena Klepfisz was born in the Warsaw Ghetto in 1941 and spent the first few years of her life there until her father smuggled her and her mother to the Aryan side in 1943. Her mother had Aryan papers and worked as a maid for a Polish family while Klepfisz was placed in a Catholic orphanage. After her father died a heroic death on the second day of the Warsaw Ghetto Uprising, April 20, 1943, Klepfisz's mother took her out of the orphanage and they survived the duration of the war in hiding in the Polish countryside.*

HASIDIM

Near the trailer park and boom boxes
blaring above each alabaster gravestone
across the street from Albertson's
with cars carrying the day's appointment of diapers,

milk, and nonfilter cigarettes,
I'd said my good-byes, stopped at a red light
before getting on Hwy 101 to Oakland.
We'd been looking at photographs,

blurry faces suspended over history's abyss,
a family who'd walked the wire
without a safety net and dropped.
I drove past the local city hall when suddenly

they came sliding toward me in black robes, hands
with square fingernails etched in night,
and for two straight seconds I didn't understand
how they'd escaped

into my living daylight
dancing around the parking lot
as though they were on to something,
Hasidim who'd grabbed the word *Yes* by the throat.

Note: *Hasidim: A branch of Orthodox Judaism founded in 18th century
Eastern Europe by Rabbi Israel Baal Shem Tov as a reaction against overly
legalistic Judaism. Hasidic teachings cherished the holiness of the unlettered
common folk, and their equality with the scholarly elite.*

T'KHINEH IN SH'VAT (SUPPLICATION IN JANUARY)

"The renewal of the moon shall be for you a beginning of new moons; it shall be for you the first among the months of the year."

—*Exodus 12:2*

Lord, if you're out there today
hesitating someplace between the branches of trees
in the interstices of black matter,
or in the dotted lines that stitch
hemispheres into a radiant globe,

I beseech you, your daughter
who reflects
from beneath the cool shadow
of her parents' death
so I may

take a breath and exhale
into a lover's ear
as you score
chronicles of the winding canal,
through and out

listening so closely, you may understand
the sorrows of the world, and by that
I don't mean the common every day stubbing,
but why a child taking piano lessons
is shot in the abdomen
by a stray bullet,

glass shattering,
or how a journalist is gunned down
in my own community,
for telling truth.

All I know
is I must find my way back to you
like a child
pushing through wild grass,
wandering far from home.

T'KHINEH IN IYAR (SUPPLICATION IN MAY)

Hear me out in less time than it takes to boil water,
you who created the People with your wisdom
and commanded us not to eat from the Tree of Knowledge,

which is not why I came
to this coffee-spilled table
near a parking lot filled with hybrid cars.

God loves the ones who speak out,
which is what I'm trying to do
talking with You while my boyfriend's
in Louisiana, and I hope you'll bless him

so he may journey back to me safely
without sitting on the tarmac for a half day
so that we might see each other
before we return to work,

and bless my step-daughter counting the days
for her below market-rate housing unit,
my son who is beginning to understand
the past does not need to dictate who he is,
and my daughter whose strength shines from her eyes
as she drives between her college dorm and Santa Rita prison.

For so many years I felt like an ox
pulling the cart of my family
along a thirsty road
making sure to avoid ruts,
and now You have breathed back
into my dry bones
so that I am a young girl sitting here
in a coffee shop near the airport
awaiting my love.

T'KHINEH IN TAMMUZ (SUPPLICATION IN JULY)

*"Of all our feelings the only one which really doesn't
belong to us is hope. Hope belongs to life, it's life
itself defending itself."*
　　　　　　　　—Julio Cortázar, *Hopscotch*

A sprig of snipped wire falls at my feet.
My neighbor recites a litany of her past dogs.

There is a tight black place behind my eyelids.
I have a crazy longing for a cigarette.

In summer, Big Sur never sleeps.
A franchise of fire marks up the sky.

My lover is gone for six days a week.
He warned me about that.

I didn't listen, protected
in his arms from my alarm clock.

Why worry about something
when it doesn't rest upon the mantlepiece?

Better to take things as they come.
As time shortens, pine needles scratch at the air.

Only sing to me, *Shekhinah*.
Your Love pools in my heart.

SH'MA YISRAEL

Hear O Israel,
from a daughter
who reads only the transliterative text of Hebrew
with glasses that need a new prescription
in a mouth that fills with saliva
from a tongue that knows not how to deliver
two-dotted vowels—

Hear O Israel
from your daughter
born in the same year
you were created,
World War II folding
charred arms around
its last hope—
Israel, the land of milk and honey—

You were the voice of my parents' generation
who planted trees along new boulevards
and carried ashes sewed
inside the hems of their skirts and trousers
to cry along the *wadis* of your limestone beds,
hugging *Exodus* by Leon Uris.

You gave them a bright torch
to carry every high holyday
for all their days
raising money and donating shoes—

a reason to drink tea
in a glass with a lump of sugar
coating their tongues with sweetness
as they stamped letters,

81

made phone calls,
argued with each other in the accent
of wherever they'd come from.

Israel, my heart is heavy
with the dreams of my parents,
this second generation daughter
who longed for a lasting peace
to fill the crevices
of your Wailing Wall
with a light of new creation.

Instead, only war and massacre,
dairy farms and steel plants
laid to rubble.
Twisted iron stabbing the earth.
And the sighs of the six million
each time another official
invokes their name.

Note: *Sh'ma Yisrael or "Hear O Israel," are the first two words of a section of the Torah (Hebrew Bible) and a centerpiece of the morning and evening Jewish prayer services. The words are a call to listen.*

FOR YAIR DALAL

Driving to Monterey
where fog caresses telephone poles,
and cypress trees bend to the waves,
where Pampas grass etches
an arc above a pod of surfers,
all their wet suits glistening black,

as your music slices a hole
through the roof of my car
without acetylene torch.
Look Ma, no hands,
a dance of sandstorms fills my head
and runs out my ears.

Sitting aloft the camel of your *oud*
there's a country vast before me,
unlike the U.S.
where my parents emigrated
as yours did from Iraq to Israel.
My soul drinks deep from desert wells

as light parses sky
into successive openings,
just watch as layers fall apart,
a veil shakes loose from the *Shekinah*
who appears like a Bedouin on the horizon,
luminous in her presence.

I want to believe there can be peace.
I want to believe that a face viewed
through the crosshairs
of a weapon

is another human being
with eyes,
nose,
tongue,
mouth,
and two ears
that listen.

Note: *Yair Dalal is an Israeli musician of Iraqi-Jewish descent. He is also a peace activist, and works to enhance understanding and communication between Arabs and Jews.*

THE CYMBALON AND THE OUD

A *cymbalon* and an *oud*
growing out from the grass
where a headstone beckons
for me to come closer.

It's my mother,
powdering herself with
Silent Night
under her arms, between her breasts.
She's busy and doesn't notice
when I sit down,
measures a tablespoon of baby oil
into her palm and smears her face,
turns into a finger painting
with her nose on a plate.

She always had a sense of humor but now
has become someone I don't recognize.

Disappears into her *boudoir*
leaving only a smell
and a trace of powder.

Gone for all those times
I needed to know what to do.
The hammer of the *cymbalon*
and the cry of the *oud*
is all she'll say.

PRAYER TO DEATH VALLEY

1.

The desert blooms gold in the spring
where I've come to make a pilgrimage
after years of living in cities.

All I hear is expanse.

Blooms yellow gold with purple mats
spreading across the desert floor
like a beautiful contagion.

I stand below sea level
on a skating pond of salt
looking out on two tectonic plates
and so want to catch it,

the way a flower struts its stuff
on a shelf of rock.

Change me.
Make me new.

2.

All I hear is expanse.

Long ago,
near Hunts Point Avenue in the Bronx,
I strolled with my doll, Judy,
along a slate pavement.

I remember how she smelled
when I first opened her box,
like a bird with the scent
of cut grass on its wing.

She had an alluvial fan of brown hair.

I loved her so much.
When her sawdust brains poured
into my hand,
my mother bought
new dolls to take her place
with clothes, and some could talk.

Impostors.

I vowed silence
until I found out
what had gone wrong,
flew back
to the only place where trees grew
in my borough, Pelham Bay Park.

3.

All I hear is expanse.

I've seen people
walk through a revolving door
to find air conditioning
on a long afternoon
exhausted by heat,
looking for water.

The dead cannot be replaced,
only remembered.

It's creation we know nothing about.

4.

Valley, uplift this daughter.
Fold together my pain.
Change me.
Make me new.

Show me the terrible place where love comes from.